Shattering the Barriers of Single Motherhood

By Sang Thi Duong

A single mom's guide to power, resilience, & the pursuit of happiness

*This book was written in honor of
my mother, Rustie Dale.
May your soul smile upon every person
who reads this book.*

I love you mom!

I dedicate this book to every Single Mother who has been making it happen, who has been holding it down, and has never given up. To the mothers who have been broken and gorilla glue just wasn't enough. To the mothers who are scared and fear what is to happen next. To the mothers who keep a smile for the kids even when it feels like everything and everyone is against them. To the mothers who stay strong on the outside and have this "thing" within them that wants more. I see you. I got you. And to my kids, who I have given my life to ... thank you for giving me daily life lessons and being the reason, I am who I am today.

I love you and one day ... I hope you understand all the why's.

THE LIFE SECTION

My Story

Allow me to set the foundation for this book with a glimpse of my past because when you know a person's background, you are able to see what they have been through, why they make the decisions they make, and how they have arrived to the person right in front of you. Every person on this planet has their own unique story darling. Even you.

I have written my story for you in bullet point style for an easier read just to give you a little peek.

My Parents: Father is Vietnamese, my mother was Caucasian. I was born in Panama City, Florida and raised in a small country town called, Huntington, Texas.

My Siblings: My sister is 7 years younger than me. My brother is 12 years younger.

My Childhood: I graduated high school in 1996 with a basketball scholarship to a private college in Missouri. I wanted to get as far away from my parents as humanly possible. You see, the summer before my senior year, my mother betrayed me and that betrayal led to my father looking me in my face while he swung in his hammock smoking a cigarette and telling me that I was a disgrace to the family, I would amount to nothing and to him, I was dead. And that the only reason I was being allowed to stay at home until I graduated was because the government told him he had to.

On the following day of my graduation in May 1996, I left. I had nowhere to go. No money. No friends. Nothing. Eventually I would live with my boss for the summer and would work all summer to pay by way to college.

The College Years: When I got to college in August, I had a $20 bill in my back pocket and no sheets for my bed. And the only things I owned were in 2 cardboard boxes and a suitcase. That was it.

In October, I was raped. I was told I was in the wrong place at the wrong time by the school administration and was told to keep my mouth shut or I would lose my scholarships.

My first semester of college was TERRIBLE. My GPA was a .50. Yes, you read that right a .50. Oh, and about that basketball scholarship. My coach told me I was too fat to be on his team. I only weighed 150 lbs. standing at 5'6" and I could box out like a boss. But, apparently, that did not matter.

As I began my 2nd semester of college, I knew something had to change. So, I decided I would go into the Air Force. I contacted the local recruiter, signed whatever papers I needed to sign. I mean, who was going to miss me. My parents were not speaking to me, I wasn't allowed to speak to my siblings -- the Air Force was a way to get an education, get paid, and be on a plan.

Well, the day I was supposed to travel to Kansas City to the do all my fancy testing ... I felt weird. And five pregnancy tests later. I was still pregnant.

I immediately called my recruiter and she told me what my options were. If I chose to have the baby, I would need to sign the rights to my baby over to someone while I was at boot camp and eventually I would be reunited OR if I chose not to have the baby, I would have to wait at least six weeks to do the physical testing required.
I was torn.

How was I going to raise a baby? How did this happen? How could I have gotten myself into this situation. I went to the father. He automatically said to get an abortion and he would pay for it. He already had a daughter and he did not want another child. BUT I was alone. How was I going to do this?

I chose to keep the baby. My son was born October 1997 and I would take him to class with me. I was determined to NOT be what society expected me to be as a single mother. All the odds were against me. And I do mean EVERY-THING!

I graduated college in December 2000 with a Bachelor of Science and my GPA was a 3.5. I took every extra class possible and did whatever I had to do to graduate.

In April 2000, I found out I was pregnant again. Only this time, I was WITH the father. During our time together, I suffered through years of physical, mental, and verbal abuse. And the worst part, I thought I did not deserve any better.

I mean, after all, my father was right. I was never going to amount to nothing. I WAS a disgrace to the family, and he reminded me of that when I graduated college in May 2000 when he *"allowed"* my mother to watch me walk across the stage.

My daughter was born in December 2000 and I would go on to experience postpartum depression. I didn't have anything to do with my daughter. I would not touch her, I would not feed, I didn't even want to be in the same room with her.

Six weeks after she was born, I became a stripper because her father was in jail and we needed money. Again. I did what I had to do.

We moved to Chicago in August of 2001 and I officially left him in the Spring of 2003. I sent my kids to Texas to live with my sister and I would go on to spend the next 6 months living out of my car. No one knew.

Oh, and I started stripping again in Spring of 2002 because the money was good, I couldn't get a job and I was constantly being told how much I was not pulling my weight around the house. I worked during the day and this is where I learned the art of conversation with men.

In January 2004, I moved into the suburbs of Chicago. Moved my kids back to me and was on a mission to start over and get my life together. And that moment happened when I was offered a job in Kansas City to work for the government. I took it. Packed up our stuff and never looked back.

It was my intention to start a new life. Raise my kids in one place to give them stability and graduate them from high school. I remember the DJ at the strip club telling me goodbye and saying, *"Oh, you will be back. They all come back."*

Little did he know. He had never met a stripper like me before. I WAS NOT GOING BACK. EVER.

After the move, I was committed to doing everything in my power to turn everything around. I had good health insurance for my kids, I was being paid well, I was blessed with a brand-new car *(since my car had been stolen on my first day in Missouri)* and I was finally seeing a light at the end of my tunnel.

Until June 2005, I woke up to 175 missed calls from my sister, my brother, and my ex. What happened? My mother died unexpectedly in her sleep. My mother gone. My best friend. Just gone. I was 27. What the fuck. She was 45. How did this happen. I was experiencing death for the first time. I was devastated.

For the next 4 months, I was a zombie. I don't remember much of what happened during that time except that the guy I was with at the time cheated on me a month after my mother passed away. Because I had no one, I took him back. He took care of my kids during my zombie state and he just let me be and did his best to get me to live my life again. In October 2005, I woke up one day and just starting living. BUT there was one caveat. I was in denial that my mother was dead.

In the spring of 2006, my guy cheated on me again. Only this time, I became the abuser. I hurt him with words, I would throw things, and my anger was out of control. Anything would set me off. And my friends called me out on it a few times. But, again, I was in denial. He deserved it because he hurt me. Right?

Fall 2006. I lost my government job. To this day, I believe she had it out for me since day one because I was a *"white"* girl with black kids - I just couldn't prove it.

Somehow, I managed to buy a house in Summer of 2007, and it was the WORST decision I ever made in my life. EVER! Why? Because I was not educated well in land of homeownership. How in the world did I buy a home for $145K when I was only making $40K at best as a Single Mother?

In the summer of 2009, I broke up with my guy. I told him I was not a good person for him, and he deserved better than how I was treating him. I no longer wanted to hurt him. He begged me not to leave. But, here's the deal. I had brainwashed him to be this way. And I knew in my heart, I was doing what was best for him...and me.

In April 2010, I met D. I was finally with a guy whom I enjoyed having sex with and did not feel like I was an object, who was not abusive to me verbally and physically, who was truly into protecting me as a woman. There was just ONE thing. He wanted kids. So, the deal was I needed to be married and before I was 36.

That did not happen. He left in May 2015.

In September 2010, I decide that the kids are no longer allowed to see their dad, he wasn't providing financial support, he was always against me, and he took the kids out of state without asking and I was just done with the drama. I let him know that if he wanted to see them, he needed to take me to court.

I also started my copywriting business.

From October 2010 through August 2011, everything was chaos. My son got suspended from school, a few months later he called me a bitch because I would not allow him to use the dishwasher to wash the dishes, and then he got caught sneaking out of the house. And I didn't know what to do, so I sent him to go live with his Godparents in Michigan. He would stay there until summer of 2013.

I lost my job at the beginning of 2012 and I kicked my copywriting business into full-time status. I also sold the house.

2013 was the worst year of my adulthood life. I was facing eviction because for the first time in my adult life - I was not able to pay my rent. My sister and her husband would bail me out.

2014 was a rebuilding year and I was laser focused on making money and getting my household affairs and money back in order. *Single Mother Academy* was officially started in the fall of 2014 and it would only evolve from there.

In 2015, the journey of self-love and truly stepping into the woman I was would begin and carry on until today. I stepped into my feminine power. I became super self-aware. I birthed my desires. I learned to love myself even more. I learned to trust women. I learned how to receive without resistance. I learned how to listen to my body as she spoke to me. I learned how to communicate with those around me in the most delightful way. I learned to use the power of daily pleasure to live a ridiculously amazing life.

In June 2017, I earned the title of Ms. Missouri Universal. Who knew I would be a pageant girl but there I was? And then in September, I earned the title of Ms. North America Universal.

And in June of 2018, my life changed forever … Stay tuned.

Dearest Single Mother

I am so glad you are here. You picked up this book because you have something burning within you that wants more. And guess what?

This is it. This is the day to start turning your desires into real life stuff. This is the day to begin shaking up your world and getting uncomfortably comfortable. This is the day you will start breaking through the barriers to live your most ridiculously ah-mazing life as a Single Mother.

This is my letter to you and the part where I tell you all the things, I desire for you to learn as you navigate through this book. This is the moment where I lay out my intentions. This is where if you are ready, to play on the playground where I fire you up about the ridiculously ah-mazing life you can create for you and your family.

This is also for you, the Single Mother (or woman), standing there reading this part of the book trying to decide if you want to buy this book or walk away. And the next few words will determine which direction you go. Talk about a lot of pressure.

No problem. Let's do this.

This book holds ONE TRUTH: ***You and only you are ultimately responsible for your happiness.***

But that truth is not where you are at this moment. This book is not going to be the complete answer to get you there, but it will definitely be a starting point. And that is the ALWAYS the first step to anything. To start.

Understanding that you have control of your own life, your own happiness, your own pleasure - does not come overnight. And it may take you three or four times to read this book before something clicks. But believe me when I tell you this -- everything happens in perfect and divine timing and you are exactly where you are supposed to be.

It's time to identify and understand every moment that has helped you arrive where you are right now.
It's time to identify and shatter every societal and personal barrier that has ever been presented before you.

Why?

Because it is damn near impossible to build a happiness playground - to become the true woman and mother you are - without first acknowledging where you are. The self-awareness you uncover on this journey about who you are, how you came to be and why you do the things you do -- is invaluable. Self-awareness is a major key to creating your life of happiness.

Have you ever believed you are not good enough?
Have you ever thought you were a bad mother?
Have you ever believed you don't deserve anything more than what you have?
Have you ever said hateful things about your own body?
Have you ever believed that you will never be loved as you want to be loved?
Have you ever thought you will be lonely forever?
Well darling. These are all bullshit.

All of those thought and beliefs have stemmed from society gibberish, our family, our friends, men we've encountered in sex or relationships -- and it's time for that to end. These thoughts and beliefs are detrimental to our lives -- they can paralyze us, damage our sense of self-love, devalue our self-worth, and hinder our ability to function within our power as Single Mothers.

Let me ask you this. When was the last time someone told you any of those things?

You are not good enough.
You are a bad mother.
You don't deserve anything more than what you have.
Your body is hideous, you should lose weight, you are ugly.
You will never be loved.
You will be lonely forever.

Hardly ever would be my guess. These things have been playing so loud in your own head that you aren't able to hear the great things about yourself. And because it has been playing on repeat for years and years - you don't even realize it is playing.

Recognizing these lies we have been telling ourselves is another key to transforming into the most fabulous version of yourself. For YOU. For your kids. For your (future) partner. In that order. When we can clearly pinpoint the root of our struggles and pain points while coming to terms that we have the power to control them -- we can absolutely change the trajectory of our lives and build the most pleasurable playground ever.

Stop beating yourself up. And, for Pete's sake, stop being another person's doormat.
Stop giving into the guilt that other's project onto you.

Stop buying your kids things just because the other kids have it and your kids nag the crap out of you.
Stop stepping away from going outside your comfort zone for fear of being alone.
Stop hanging out with people who don't value your brilliance.
Stop accepting less than you deserve.
Stop doing things that do not bring you happiness or pleasure.
Stop feeding your mind with negative garbage.
Just stop.

Every Single Mother story is different, every Single Mother's life is different - yet every Single Mother ultimately desires the same. **Happiness.**

In this book.... you are going to get a glimpse of my life as a Single Mother over the past 20+ years. I am going to share my truths. My triumphs. My downfalls. My real life. Some of it, you may be able to relate to, some of it you may not. Some of it you will cause you to raise your eyebrows, some of it will may make you cry. Some things I did you may agree with and some things, you just won't. Whichever person you are. It is OK.

I value to be truthful with you and it is my intention to share the REAL truths of life behind the doors of Single Motherhood. I am going to be really REAL about who I am and how I came to be this woman who wrote you this book.

Your life is ridiculously ah-mazing. Your life is one incredible journey from one beautiful place to another. It is not about looking in the rearview mirror to continuously revisit pain that brings you down every single time. It is not a hamster wheel where you keep running and running and not getting where you want. It is not an intersection you keep returning to over and over again.

Your life will not look like mine or your neighbor's or your co-worker's. Your life is your design.

And here is another truth: ***It is not going to be a smooth sailing journey.***

There will be more bumps on the journey. There will be tears. There will be anger. There will love. There will be discovery of self.

Because if you are exactly where you are right now...365 days from today -- how will you feel?

This journey you are about to embark upon -- is not microwaveable. You are not able to pop it in the microwave like a bag of popcorn and tada...it's ready. This will be an ongoing journey. You will try out some different tools and techniques and, while some may feel good to you, others may not tickle your fancy as much. You will uncover the tools that fit you perfectly and you will find others that send you for the hills.

Oh. And this truth. ***You will fail.***

You will fall off the wagon during this journey. You will tell yourself you are OK. You will revert back to an old thought or belief. You will fall into a crevice of crap. And it's OK. This is life. It happens.

Once you marry the truth that you are in control of your life and happiness - you will get up, put on that outfit that makes you feel fabulous -- and try again. And you will keep getting up until being in control feels more natural than chaos and confusion. Your resilience to overcome barriers will strengthen.

You are not meant to be a caterpillar forever darling. You are meant to be more than slowly trekking along in life inch by inch. You are destined to fall into your cocoon of self-discovery and emerge as a beautiful butterfly who can see beyond the struggles, who has the power and resilience to take on life with love and pleasure to live your most amazing and ridiculous life.

This is what I tell the Single Mothers I speak to, who email me. who message me on Facebook or Instagram.

Because of you -- this book was born. I have talked to many Single Mothers and time and time again they would say, *"Sang, I can't wait for you to write a book."*

And I would shrug it off. And then it hit me. What if.

What if I FINALLY write a book where I share my stories of how I have struggled. What if I share the dark moments where I felt like I wanted to die? What if I share the hard questions my kids asked and how I responded? What if I share how I have bad days and the voice in my head takes over from when my father would tell me I was not good enough. What if I could reach thousands of Single Mothers and give them a glimpse of hope and empower them to have what I did not. What if I share my own reflections of my life and how it has strengthened my relationship with my kids?

What if I share that I love myself more than anyone else? I am at a peaceful place in my life and I live a ridiculously ah-mazing life. And how I love myself even when I make bad decisions. How is this even possible.

Because I love myself so hard and I have a complete understanding that I am in control of my life. I am in control of my happiness. I am in control of my pleasure. I am in control of my power.

Today is not over yet and tomorrow is a new day. Every moment is a moment to just start. You have a chance to begin the journey to live your best life right now.

I will share with you the tools and resources that I have used to overcome the daily struggles of Single Motherhood. And by sharing these stories, it is my hope that this book will help you make more empowered choices as a Single Mother. I hope you will relate to my stories, and more than anything, I hope you give your inner woman permission to break free.

YOU ARE MY PURPOSE.

How to get the most out of this book

First things first. Stop and Reflect

I was sitting here looking around my apartment because I was in a funk earlier today. Feeling down. Feeling less than. Feeling unloved. Feeling like my world was crumbling.

You see. For the past two weeks, things have not been all peaches and cream – heck more like Cheetos and pickles with a side of all fat mayonnaise.

Over my last 30-awesome years – I have had over 35 jobs. I have done everything from car detailing to bartending to retail store manager to paralegal to cheerleading coach to nanny to you name it.

Nothing stuck. Obviously.

Instead. I became a Queen of all trades and I was deemed the lady who could do it all. I mean I could, right? Today while sitting on the couch, I felt the shift. Something is happening, and I cannot explain it. But I know in my heart the earth beneath my feet is about to shake.

And you want to know why? Because I live a ridiculously amazing life.

I have raised (and still raising) a black son from cradle to college to be a human who makes the world a better place with his genius, his ability to twerk, and his patience with me as his mother. And if you don't think that is a challenge – remember I am his Asian mother. What the hell do I know about being a black man? #LetThatSoakIn

I am raising one of the most confident, strong-willed, go make your dreams a reality natural hair growing daughter to chase her dreams. And, yet again, I am her Asian mother – with very white hair. What the hell do I know about managing 4B-4C natural hair? #LetThatSoakIn

I am creating a community for Single Mothers to thrive, live, be loved, and honor who they are from the inside out alongside other Single Mothers who cherish them, support them and never knock them down. #SingleMother20Years

And I have connected with some of the strongest, hard-working, loving mothers the world needs to know. #SingleMomsAreHeros

What could I possibly be sitting on this couch in a funk?

Everything I've ever wanted is right here…. in front of me.

My world is unraveling before my eyes – my dream is coming true – my life is great … I created this amazing life.

~ Facebook Post: 9.23.16

I wrote that post and it was so true. Everything began to shift and shift hard after that day. If I had not taken a moment to just pause and reflect. We may not be here today. Life is busy. I sooooo get that. And if you are anything like me, you go, go, go, go -- and then down time is needed. I get that too.

But, seriously, when was the last time you stopped to take credit for EVERYTHING you have done in your life up to this very moment (and then said – HELL YEAH, I DID THAT)?

Play on the Power & Pleasure Playground

Here is what I know to be true. You have all the answers. Not me, not your friends, not this book. This book is designed to take you on a path to shattering the barriers of Single Motherhood that are blocking you from designing your best life as a Single Mother and as a woman.

Within the walls of this book, I will invite to you the power & pleasure playground. As with any invitation, you can RSVP - NO. And that is OK too. Perhaps it is not time for that exercise just yet. The playground is simply designed to enhance your power and pleasure for your happiness.

I highly recommend you play in the playground in the moment, even if it feels a tad bit uncomfortable -- because in order to expand our comfort zone, we must get uncomfortable.

Power, pleasure and happiness live in the now and have long-lasting effects. Often, we wait until we have lost XX lbs., or until we have had time to think things through -- then you know what happens. NOTHING. We forget. I strongly urge you to act immediately.

Feel free to revisit a particular area of the playground. Visit frequently if you must. Your inner woman is forever evolving and changing. Today your pleasure may be different than the one you had last week. Learn to listen to what your inner woman wants - she never lies. I promise.

Permission Granted to Live YOUR Best Life

As you navigate through the playground, it is super important to remember that every Single Mother's journey through life is way different. Some places on the playground may come as easy as eating an entire bag of Oreos in one sitting and some of them may seem as perplexing as rock climbing sideways.

Either way. You have my permission to design and live your best life. Not the live that others want you to live. Not the life that society thinks you should live.

YOUR LIFE. YOUR TERMS. YOUR DESIRES.

Allowing yourself to expand power and pleasure as a Single Mother is a super courageous act darling, no matter how big or small. And what I hope you learn is that there is no right or wrong way to do thing this Single Mom thing. You got this.

I mean. By simply having this book in your hands or on your screen, you have done everything just right.

Create Your Own Single Mother Posse

One of the most common things I hear Single Mothers say is that they have NO support, NO one to talk to, NO one that gets it. Or there is a sense of shame and judgement that is taken on from the piercing stares, whispers, or stories made up by everyone around you...about you.

One of the most effective way to survive this Single Motherhood life is to have a community of women to support you. Which is why I extend the invitation to creating your own society of Single Mothers with whom you can talk to, share stories, lift one another up, give praise to one another, able to walk with you through whatever life happening is going down right now -- and provide a safe place free of shame and judgement.

Your Posse has your back. Gives you praise. Compliments you. Loves on you when you need it and gives you that tough love. They get you and they want to see you happy. Some days will require emergency calls to a Posse member who can support your emotions or who can just listen to you talk through your thoughts. Your Posse will hold sacred space for you as you desire. Allow them to support you and the hardest part of all -- receive their love and support with open arms.

Single Motherhood does not have to be a lonely place or an isolated experience. After all, you are creating the life you desire remember.

About my style

I keep it real. No sugar coating. If I wanted to sugar coat things, I would have been a baker darling. This is **REAL** life. With **REAL** stories. About **REAL** events. This, my friend, is **REAL** talk. I am asking you hard questions. I am poking you to looking within. I am asking you to be honest with yourself. Because I believe when we are honest with ourselves, we are able to be in love with who we are, and we are able to release the shackles that have held our self-love captive.

I mean -- who else is willing to talk about what really goes down as a Single Mother. And be that friend who is going to tell you the hard truths. I am here for you to find your power, love yourself unconditionally, and live your best life. I am here to listen to you. Lift you up. Wipe your tears. Comfort you. And then release you to out into the world for you to fulfill your desires.

And while it may seem like it is you against the world, it really is you against you sweet darling. And if there is anything, I want you to know...**KNOW THIS:**

I got you. I am with you.
I am on your side. I believe in you.

Chapter 1: Redefining Single Motherhood

Allow me to share the tiniest secret that packs the most power.

The way to getting your happiness starts with finding the happiness **where you are.**

Most of us, Single Mothers, have extreme difficulty accepting the beauty of who we are. For so long, we as women, have been taught to dislike our bodies, feed ourselves

hate-talk, feel as though we are never enough -- and we are in
a constant state of disapproval of ourselves and our lives.

But I am here to challenge you to put self-doubt, self-
loathing, judgement, and negative self-talk aside and begin to
define Single Motherhood however the hell you want to. And
a key step in becoming the best version of you -- is to find
pleasure and happiness from where you are right now.

Often times we delay our happiness. We put our desires,
dreams, and goals on the backburner until we feel it is the
right time or we feel worthy enough.

But the thing with that is this...

Our worthiness comes in small pockets in our lives. We
give. We give. We give. And we believe that we are not worthy
of happiness. But we hold to that small inkling of hope.

We become the *"One day I'll _____________________ (fill in
the blank with your desire)."*

"When the kids are _________, I'll do _____________________"

...That's when I will be happy.

But can I let you in on another little secret, darling.

YOU ARE WORTHY.

YOU DESERVE ALL THAT YOU DESIRE.

Yes. You. Single Mom. Single Mama. Single Mother.

I remember when I found out I was pregnant. I took FIVE pregnancy tests to make sure and as I stood there looking at FIVE positive pregnancy tests -- I was frozen. What was I going to do?

I decided to keep the baby -- and let me tell you -- I had no idea the odds were so stacked against me -- as a Single Mother. I was a freshman in college, I had no money, no job, no family support, no true friends yet, and I was going to have a baby. OK. Cool. I got this. I will survive.

Yet -- every I looked -- the world was against me.

Single Mothers can't work because they will always miss work.
Single Mothers won't graduate from college OR be able to get a decent paying job.
Single Mothers will always live on welfare.
Single Mothers are hoes.
Single Mothers are looking for someone to save them.

Now. Single mothers come in all forms. *Never married. Divorced. Widowed. By choice.*

I remember when I was conducting a survey and I had asked three questions:

1. What are your top 3 most challenging things about being a single mother?
2. What is the #1 thing you need the most help with?
3. What is something you needed and looked for resources but could not find what you were looking for?

And a lady I knew answered like this, *"Sang, first of all. I want you to know that I am not a single mother because I had my children out of wedlock. I am single mother because I am a widow."*

Ummmmm ok. Thank you, lady. At first, I felt as if she was taking a jab at me and I became angry. That anger turned into curiosity and then I realized this is, yet, another element of Single Motherhood that society has played a part in creating. You see, I realized that no matter how a person became a Single Mother, I stand for you. Because when I received her answers to those three questions, they were the same answers as the mothers who had their children out of wedlock.

I am not here to tell you if you are Single Mother or not. If you identify as a Single Mother, that is your prerogative. I just know **I AM** a Single Mother and I have been for over 200K+ hours and going. I respect your choice to call yourself whatever your heart desires.

"Single Mother" comes with all kinds of public shaming. No group is as linked to poverty in the American mind as single mothers. For decades, politicians, journalists and scholars have diligently scrutinized the reasons women have children out of wedlock and do not marry.

In 2015, Jeb Bush was asked about chapter in his book which he blamed the "irresponsible conduct" of births to unmarried women on a flagging sense of community ridicule and shaming. He stated, *"My views have evolved over time, but my views about the importance of dads being involved in the lives of children hasn't changed at all. In fact, since 1995 ... this book was a book about cultural indicators [and] the country has moved in the wrong direction. We have a 40-plus percent out-of-wedlock birth rate…. It's a huge challenge for single moms to raise children in the world that we're in today and it hurts the prospects, it limits the possibilities of young people being able to live lives of purpose and meaning."* As a southern girl, through and through. ***Bless his heart.***

Here is how I decided to live my truth

Single Motherhood is whatever I defined it to be.

You teach others how to treat you as a Single Mother.
You decide if you will allow others to project their Single Mother judgements upon you.
You set the boundaries to protect your time, your space and your sanity while being a Single Mother.
You make decisions that best for you -- as a Single Mother.

Each day you have the opportunity to wake up with a *"let me wallow in my life sadness"* or with a *"I run this place and nothing and no one is going to stand in my way"* kinda attitude. Which one will you choose?

Power & Pleasure Playground

Dispel the beliefs.

Make a list of all the societal beliefs you know about being a Single Mother. All of the cultural conditioning, all the unspoken behaviors of Single Mothers. Take note of how you are *supposed* to behave as a Single Mother. Your list may include things like, *"I'm on welfare,"* or *"I have kids by more than one man,"* or *"Nobody wants to be with a single mother because she's always looking for a handout."*

As you are listing these beliefs, you are bringing light to the long-held assumptions and societal teachings. What you jot down may surprise you. Once you have the list, go back through the list and ask yourself - whether it is true or not - does this define who I am as a mother or a woman?

Do you presume that you cannot be a Single Mother AND happy? Single Mother AND have money? Single Mother AND be loved?

Make this list and place it into a drawer. In a few months - after you have had time to digest this book. See if any of those beliefs have diminished.

Stamp of Approval.

I would bet that you don't even notice how much you disapprove of yourself and your life. As Single Mothers, we continuously have the disapproval reel on repeat which says, *"I should have done this..." "I didn't do this good enough" "I will never be able to afford this" "I will always be alone and single,"* and so on.

With just a subtle shift in language, you can add approval and positive forecasting on your decisions.

Try saying instead:

"I did this to the best of my abilities and that is enough"
"I did it this way because at the time, it was the right decision
  for me"
"I am worthy of all things and soon this will be mine"
"I deserve love and it will come to me right on time"

Once you start becoming more aware of those devilish thoughts that are whirling around inside, you will be able to ward them off as they are not welcome because you accept where you are.

As soon as you trust yourself,
you will know how to live.
~ Johann Wolfgang von Goethe

Chapter 2: Embrace Your Inner Goddess
(then play with her)

I've always had high aspirations. Even as a little girl, I was always trying to go against the grain, and I was silently competitive with others. I always wanted to be the best at everything, but I was never vocal about my level of competitiveness since I was taught not to speak or show emotion.

A few years ago, I was going through family photos and I came across an essay I wrote when I was a senior in high school. When I read it, I smirked I've always been brilliant with a survivor mentality -- I just did not realize it.

Here is the essay:

"There once was a crow, half dead with thirst, that came upon a glass which had once been full of water; but when the crow put its beak into the mouth of the glass, he found that only very little water was left in it, and that he could not reach far enough to get it. He tried and he tried, but, at last, had to give up in despair. Then a thought came to him, and he took a pebble and dropped it into the glass. Pebble after pebble, he dropped into that glass. Finally, the water was near him and he was able to quench his thirst and save his life."

The theme of the anecdote was that the crow had given up physically but not mentally. The crow was determined to get to that water, and he knew he could not give up. Finally, after he was able to reach the water, he knew that he had succeeded. If the crow had thought of this idea but felt he was too stupid or too dumb to make anything work, then he would have died of thirst. He had enough confidence in himself and enough determination to succeed, and that he did.

As Americans, we must remember that America is the land of unlimited possibilities and with our expectations set high, we are sure to achieve anything we want.

My vision for America is for the people to have the ability to achieve their goals by having enough confidence and determination to reach them and to be proud of themselves whether they succeed or not. What is vision? Vision may be something in a dream or an object of imagination, but I see vision as an art of seeing.

There are four kinds of people in America, those who make things happen, those who watch things happen, those who wonder what happened, and those who don't know anything that happened. By having confidence and determination, there will only be one kind of person in America: those who make things happen.

Every American will follow his own direction and be the architect of his own fortune. The minds of the people will create themselves, springing up under every disadvantage and making their way through every obstacle.

Most people will live and die with their music still unplayed. They never attempted to try. Why? Because they lack confidence. Confidence is as far from conceit as the desire to earn a decent living is remote from greed. The people of America will have the confidence in oneself and in one's abilities.

In an interview, Albert Einstein is reported to have advised young people to follow this bit of wisdom, "Do not try to be a person of success but try to be a person of value. The successful person takes more out of life that they put in it; while the person of value gives more to life than they take out of it."

The people of America will work with ability and determination as if it were the last day of their life and they will initiate self-improvement as if they were going to live a hundred years.

There is one quality more important that "know how" and we cannot accuse the people of any undue amount of it. This is "know what" by which we determine not only how to accomplish our purposes, but what out purposes are to be. People today do not go out and achieve their goals because they fear failure. There is a saying that states: "Those who fail never attempted to try. If you do not at least try, then you have failed."

Competition can have a strong effect on how you reach your goals. You learn that it becomes most powerful when you compete with yourself and when you learn from your failures.
The people of my generation will help make this vision a reality by having the confidence and determination to achieve their goals. They will go after what they want and if they fall short, they will try again or go after something better. Whatever goals the people of my generation attempt, they will succeed whether they fail or not. Simply because they have made an effort to reach their goal rather than not trying at all.

I leave you with this last statement: Be what you are. This is the first step toward becoming better than you are.

Written by me in 1996 for the VFW Essay Scholarship Contest

After I read this, I could not help but think, what if I had believed in myself as much as I believed in this essay. I knew who I was then, but I had no idea how to shed the barriers to step into my greatness.

And what I know to be true is that the most powerful characteristic you can have is to know who you are, what you stand for, what you desire, what grinds your gears, how you want to live, how you want to feel -- because when you have an inkling of those pouring through your veins -- the momentum will carry you through.

When you know who you are and what you stand for -- *you have a foundation to live a ridiculously ah-mazing life.*

When you know what you desire -- *you begin to plant seeds.*

When you know what grinds your gears -- *the better you are able to self-manage your emotions.*

When you know how you want to live -- *you find ways to make it happen without playing the victim role.*

When you know how you want to feel -- *you will do whatever it takes to keep that feeling.*

As women, we often can't articulate what we want because we are taught never to give our happiness or desires any attention, energy, or even make it a priority. And, most times, when our happiness appears before us, we can't even recognize it.

So why does having happiness get such a bad rap with Single Mothers? If a Single Mothers are seen wanting too much or are aiming too high, society takes her down with their snarky and degrading comments. As if being a Single Mother is equivalent to wearing the scarlet letter A.

Well I have news for society. SCREW YOU.

Single Mothers can have everything they desire and then some because, to me, without aspirations for wanting more, being more, having more -- you are stuck in the cycle society wants you in. And what stinks is that I have seen the societal stigma way too much.

When I hear a Single Mom is suffering from apathy and just doesn't have the desire to want more, do more, or be more -- I simply want to run to her and give her mouth-to-mouth and inject life into her again. Because what I know is that society, friends, and even family have broken her mental mindset and she feels she is not deserving of such great things or even allowed to be happy.

And I am here to tell you. YOU CAN HAVE WHAT YOU WANT. YOU CAN BE WHATEVER YOU WANT. YOU CAN DO WHATEVER YOU WANT.

You should aspire to be on your own personal level of excellence to be the best that you can be. You should aspire to have the most ridiculously amazing life you can get in terms of fulfillment and happiness and peace. And then when it comes to material things -- sign up for the best there is -- and moving forward, this should be your default attitude about everything in life.

Just picture me as Jane Fonda in 1985 saying, *"Come on Ladies! You can do it! Feel the Burn."* The only exception is I do it in jeans and sparkly heels. I don't give you a glimpse of my lifestyle to tease you or to make you feel bad. I just want to light a fire under your ass and let you know what is possible because in my opinion you actively wanting the best -- is simply a fire burning within you that needs to be fanned to get your butt in gear and make shit happen.

Desire vs. Goals

Desires live within you and the entire purpose of our being. Each day is a day to unfold your desires one by one and continue to evolve into the woman you are. Desires are not frivolous -- it between you and what is greater than you. Your desires are not meaningless -- your desires can take you higher. No matter how small or big.

When you give your desires attention -- you give it life and the will to transform as you wish. Desires can take you to a place you may never have imagined. Desires are powered by the essence of you.

Goals are merely tangible things you can attain.

Maybe you want to lose 5 pounds.
Maybe you want to change careers.
Maybe you want to get a raise.

Those are all pretty tangible because you know HOW to make them happen. It's a matter of taking the steps. And the issue that comes up with a goal, you judge yourself wrong if you don't have it already or you don't attain it in a certain amount of time.

With a desire, it unfolds YOU because you are never actually there but you're there. You are in the process of getting there and attaining that feeling of that desire is what is longing within you. You want the feeling that goes with the desire you yearn for.

When your desires make you salivate, you know you've touched a point of elevation. The point where you can taste your desires, smell your desires, inhale the sheer fragrance of what you've ultimately wanted....and it's the next step that will take your desires to an even higher vibration.

Pleasure & Power Playground

Your Desire List.

Get out a piece of paper (not your journal) and a pen. It's time to create your ultimate desire list. On your paper, put your heart's desire - from wearing lacy black panties to a hot bubble bath, a date with a man who opens the door and has manners, a weekend alone to just do nothing, sex in an elevator, eating ice cream for breakfast, your bills paid two months in advance, to get a raise at work and more vacation time -- absolutely ANY - THING you want.

Then. Once you have finished your list -- I invite you to post it in a place that you pass by frequently -- perhaps your bedroom door, your bathroom mirror, in your closet -- This way you see it every day.

Mark your calendar one month from the day you write it. Check your list -- update it. Cross off what you received or maybe you have more desires to add. And whenever you receive something on your list - next to that desire - write, *"Thank you, ____________"* to whoever responsible for bringing your desires true.

I promise, you will be quite surprised how quickly your desires come true and how much your desires begin to expand.

Start a Journal.
Stating your Intentions out loud a writing them down on paper can confirm things and make them happen. It's a way of stating your intentions to the universe and letting the universe know your hopes and dreams and wishes and giving them an actual concrete form.

"You are Fabulous" Mirror.
Choose one mirror in your home and deem it the "You are Fabulous" mirror.

Here is how it works darling: when you pass by this mirror you must choose to see all the beautiful things: what you love, what makes you amazing, your accomplishments -- this is not a place of criticism. As women, we often look in mirrors with disdain and pick out flaws. We tend to abuse ourselves with our own mind and feed our bodies body shaming words. We disapprove of how our hair looks, if our eyebrows are not perfect, or that little belly pooch we despise.

"You are Fabulous" Mirror -- extended version

For this one, you will need to have a mirror in a private location in your home -- and you will more than likely want to do this when the kids are asleep or gone. I also recommend a journal for this one.

Here how the extended version works: take off all your clothing - *if you need to stay in your bra and panties you can, but if you want to push your boundaries - get completely nude* - and stand in front of the mirror. Find one body part and focus on that body part for FIVE minutes.

What does this body part do for you?

How has this body part helped you get to where you are today?

What do you love about this body part?

Remember, this is not a place of negativity or criticism. I encourage you to increase your time as you get the hang of things. Your time you choose to honor your body, is your call.

Love your body. Love your mind. Love your words. You are love, darling.

Chapter 3:
Pleasure as a Superpower

Pleasure.

When I first heard the word. I thought of something sexual. I mean. What else was pleasure if not sex. And, to me, sex was everything BUT pleasure.

Pleasure is about looking within -- to see what feels good -- and doing it. What if you created a life where pleasure was a daily rule rather than an exception? What would that look like for you?

First, let's define pleasure.

Pleasure

Definition: *noun. a feeling of happy satisfaction and enjoyment.*

Pleasure can be a loaded term. Pleasure can be misunderstood (just like Single Mothers). Often it is associated with sex, but when we break pleasure down to its true essence - pleasure is rather simple. It is no more or no less than experiencing life through our senses.

Pleasure is a way of life.
Pleasure is power we all have within us, yet we have been taught to turn our heads away from.
Pleasure is a taboo kinda word.
Pleasure is happiness.
Pleasure is bliss.

I want you to feel this euphoria of pleasure.

When I uncovered my pleasure and created my pleasure wheel -- my entire life shifted. Pleasure is now a part of my daily life -- it is a non-negotiable. You know how you can know something like the back of your hand? That's how well I want you to know what brings and gives you pleasure. I want you to know what it looks like, what it feels like, what it tastes like and how it sounds.

As a matter of fact, I want you to know more about your pleasure than the back of your hand because THAT is how much POWER your pleasure can give you. Think of your pleasure like a bottomless well of water -- it's never ending. It's always going to be there for you.

Where did I uncover my pleasure and sensuality? Simple.

Mama Gena's School of Womanly Arts

In 2012, I began hosting Vision Board Brunches at the beginning of every year and then in 2015, I transformed it into, *"Create Your Happy Plan."* The happy plan was about showing more love, being more present, and living life filled with family, experiences, and connecting with women who make a difference.

However, in 2015 I found myself a tad bit overwhelmed. Clients were happy, I was happy, everything was copacetic. Then, like a freight train, a series of unfortunate events happened and the happiness I was experiencing ceased in a snap. I slipped into a mini stagnant state and I did not want to be around anyone.

I found myself drowning and I was not sure how I was going to be able pull myself above the water. Then you know those stories where people tell you -- it just happened.

Well. That is what happened to me. After several weeks of my wallowing in my bed, not wanting to get up -- just pull the covers over my head and let me be. BUT. It was if a bolt of lightning struck me in the bed. My mind instructed my body to bolt out of bed and all I could feel was there was some sort of energetic wildfire within me.

I walked into the bathroom. Looked at myself dead in the eyes and said, *"I deserve to be happy. I deserve to live a great life. I deserve to just be me. Now pull yourself together and make it happen."*

And in January 2016, when I attended Mama Gena's Experience in New York City - I had set an intention to let whatever happen to happen - I was opening myself up to possibility and opportunity. On the first day, I was in awe. I felt welcomed, I felt loved, I felt seen, I felt radiant, I felt like everything that was happening was supposed to happen.

And then, I was introduced to pleasure.

Pleasure. Oh yes. Pleasure. I'll take two please. Thanks.

Pleasure feels like you're on top of the world.
Or feels euphoric like the taste of *"fresh from the oven"* brownies.

Or like the feeling of butterflies fluttering when you are trying something scary exciting.

Pleasure had become the most erotic thing in my life, and it had NOTHING TO DO WITH SEX.

During Mastery, I realized that I had always known my pleasure. I knew how to use my pleasure and sensuality to get what I desired, feel good and create this ridiculously ah-mazing life. I had been practicing the art of pleasure my entire life -- I just did not know it.

I encourage every Single Mother and woman who reads this book to be extremely fluent in the language of your own pleasure. I want you to own your sensuality because when own your sensuality -- the world is yours. If you are sensually aware of your pleasure, I promise you darling, you will walk with a little more pop, you will be more confident, and you will enjoy life more.

Because, for me, when I am in tune with my pleasure...

> I sashay the earth with a special kinda confidence swag
> I smile because I know I am living my best life
> I hit the pause button on life and sloooow the F down
> I feel fulfilled
> I feel unstoppable
> I say NO to things that don't bring me pleasure
> I watch the haters, the talk behind my back peeps, and I
> just smile because they have no idea what my pleasure is
> I conjure up my desires in the most delicious way possible

Knowing what brings you pleasure makes you an unstoppable woman. Every ounce of bliss, joy, laughter, and answers you have ever searched for -- you have the power to give yourself pleasure which results in power.

I have made pleasure a foundational element in my life, my relationships my family, and my business. If something doesn't feel good, it does not happen. Simple as that.

All you have to do is choose to feel good. Just like happiness is a choice -- pleasure is a choice. Pleasure is how you define it for you. For one Single Mother, pleasure may be waking up 30 minutes early every day to sit in her comfy chair and journal while she sips on her favorite hot beverage. For another Single Mother, pleasure may be lacing up her running shoes and running every morning.

Pleasure comes from giving yourself permission to explore your pleasure without guilt.

Are you ready to uncover your pleasure and unleash your power darling?

Power & Pleasure Playground

Create Your Pleasure Wheel

Grab a piece of paper and write down all the things that bring you pleasure. Pleasure has no size. How are your desire different from pleasure? Pleasure is a state of mind where you are in charge of saying yes or no.

Here are a few ideas shared from other single mothers to get your pleasure wheel turning...

Play the song that every time you hear it -- you are ready to drop it like it hot (or sing from the top of your lungs Send your kids to daycare and call in sick.

Before bed, you take a nice hot bath - or perhaps a Cleopatra bath

Write a few handwritten cards to people who have touched your life

Stop what you are doing, go get a pedicure, turn your phone off or to silent -- and relax

Watch a movie that gets you inspired. Erin Brockovich is a great one #SingleMother

Light a candle, grab your soft blanket, grab that magazine or book you've been wanting to read

Write love notes to yourself and hide them in drawers and bags, inside the refrigerator, in your suitcases, and even under pillows. Surprise yourself with love

The next time you get of the shower to put on lotion, turn on some slow music and apply the lotion to the tempo of the music

Have a bedroom picnic

Set a gorgeous blanket on the bed and sprinkle it with rose petals or confetti.

Light a few candles – then light 5 more.

Play music that is soothing and relaxing.

Set out some delicious treats that make your palate excited.

Eat everything with your hands.

And this…. take your sweet, sweet time and become one with your serene playground for as long as your heart desires.

Chocolate Always Give Good Pleasure

Buy a bar of chocolate that satisfies your taste buds. Over super low heat add a splash of milk to the saucepan. Add a few chunks of the chocolate and stir with a wooden spoon.

When the chocolate has melted, add a few more pieces as you wish, and a tad bit more milk until you get a nice, smooth, warm, gooey flow of chocolate.

Serve in a cute bowl with a can of whipped cream.

And to top off your delicious chocolate, add your favorite dippable delights (a few ideas: strawberries, cubes of pound cake, warmed croissant, animal crackers, graham crackers)

Have a Cleopatra Bath

You may have heard of Cleopatra. She ruled Egypt. She was beautiful. She walked the Earth in pleasure. And she bathed in milk and honey.

And as cliché as it may sound, bathing in milk and honey is an exceptional way to get **soft, supple skin** – all over your body. The lactic acid in milk is **very exfoliating**, and honey is **softening, moisturizing, and all-around beautifying**.

The key is to use full-fat milk (or powdered milk) and pure honey. Full-fat milk will not only exfoliate the skin, but it will also moisturize.

(Source: Unknown)

Chapter 4: Self-Care is NOT Selfish

IT IS ALL ABOUT YOU.

YES. YOU.

And the best example of this is when you are flying, and the
flight attendant tells you:

*"Should the cabin lose pressure, oxygen masks will drop from
the overhead area. Please place the mask over your own
mouth and nose before assisting others."*

Self-care is taking care of you so you can take of the family.

Prioritizing yourself. Slowing down. Getting enough sleep. Drinking water. Eating whole foods. Moving your body.

When was the last time you did something JUST FOR YOU? When was the last time you did something FOR THE FIRST TIME?

We all tend to slip into this mode of treating lie as if we have another one hanging in the closet.

Later is NOW.
Like.
RIGHT NOW.

Let's do a little math problem, shall we?

Grab a pen and a piece of paper and a calculator
Multiply your age x 365
Subtract that number from 27, 375 (that's the average life-span +/- a few days)

I probably have _________ days left.

Want to know how many years?

Divide that number by 365.

I probably have _______ years left.

"Live each day as if it's your last …. Because one day you'll be right."

Self-care is not selfish. Let me repeat.

SELF-CARE IS NOT SELFISH.

We both know that being a Single Mom is hard. There's a reason why when I speak at events or to my posse of friends -- I mention self-care. Self-care is about taking care of your mental and physical health and hello -- keeping your sanity as a Single Mother. Because we both know that you have a million and one things to get done and when you run yourself to the point of exhaustion -- nothing gets done.

And then what happens.

You get mad at yourself for not doing enough. For not getting it done. You pull out the boxing gloves and start beating yourself up. Then, eventually, you get up and start tackling the list with anger, resentment, sadness and it's just not a good feeling.

And then the cycle repeats.

It's time to SHATTER THE BARRIER that self-care is a bad thing.

And before you give me the *"no time or money"* for self-care -- pump the brakes. It is, by far, my favorite excuse to hear and I promise you -- I SEE YOU.

You don't have to spend money to put self-care into your daily practice. And I am going to give you the cliché statement, *"Investing in you by practicing self-care is, by far, the most important thing you can do for your family and YOU."*

My philosophy is this -- when you know and love yourself completely and intimately, physically, emotionally, spiritually, sensually -- you have a competitive advantage.

Power & Pleasure Playground

Take a "Sick" Day

As a Single Mother, time is always escaping us. When I was working a full-time job, 2 part-time jobs and volunteering 40+ hours a week -- time was so valuable. And I was known to take a "sick" day.

And on that "sick" day, I would take care of the millions of things that were on my to-do list that I just could not get done if I was at work all day. It made me feel good that

I gave myself permission to do what I needed to do to get shit done. Allow yourself a day without worry. A day with simple trust and an inner knowing of the truth that it's all going to be ok.

Eat Slowly. Take a Moment and Breathe.

For your next meal or snack I want you to slooooooow things down. I want you to take your time eating your food and really savor the taste.

I want you to sit at the table or somewhere that is not your "normal" on the go spot. As a matter of fact, I want everything you do to be the opposite of what you would normally do.

Use a real plate. Use a real glass. Put your phone away. No distractions. Make it a moment to sit, eat, and just be. What do you hear? What do you see? How do you feel? Would you like to add real flowers? Would like to light a candle? What is in your pleasure?

Then I want you to get into the habit of eating slowly and more attentively more often. You will be amazed at the difference it is for your mind, your body, and your happiness.

Declutter One Space a Day.

I want to pick ONE space. Just one. It could be your fingernail polishes, your panty drawer, or your car. You decide.

Set a timer so that you don't get whisked away into declutter land and we have to send in an army to get you back.

By decluttering space, you are removing what is no longer needed to open up space for what you desire. You can ask yourself the infamous Marie Kondo question, *"Does this spark joy?"* or ask, *"Does this bring me pleasure?"* or you may need to ask, *"When was the last time I used this?"*

You are committing to having a clear mind and clear space which is a starting point to loving your life, your space, and enjoying what is important.

Media Detox

Have you ever been on Facebook and then 2 hours later you're like, *"WHAT THE HELL?"*

I know. I have been there too.

Whatever your time sucking social media vice is, you can start with ONE. Email. Instagram. Facebook. Pinterest. Snapchat. Pick one and go from there.

Maybe you want to unfollow/unfriend people. Maybe you want to unsubscribe from emails you never read. Maybe you want to delete that account entirely. Maybe you want to limit your time on that platform.

Do whatever you like. The purpose is to be mindful of the time you spend on these platforms and give yourself some "healthy" boundaries. By doing a media detox, you are reducing your stress levels, you're creating a clearer mind for better sleep, you're not getting sucked into negative comments or rants -- you are focused on the quality of life and setting intentions of how you want to spend your time.

Baby Steps Self-Care Challenge

Come up with a FUN and TINY self-care goal that you can realistically and happily commit to. Something that will give you pleasure, and it doesn't have to be food or exercise related.

It can be ANYTHING health or body related.

Your goal could be: *"I will wear matching bra and panties every day this week because it makes me feel confident!"* ... *"I will rub my favorite lotion on my legs after every shower nice and slow because I love how to smells against my skin."* ... *"I will drink cucumber/lemon water every morning before breakfast."* ... *"I will spend 10 minutes a day writing freely in my journal for the rest of the month!"*

Think SIMPLE. Think: REALISTIC. Think: FUN.

20 Self-Care Things You Can Do

1. Take a dance break. Turn up your favorite booty shaker and get busy.
2. Watch a movie without distractions. Just be in the space.
3. Read a fiction book or short story that you can totally lose yourself in.
4. Journal your thoughts with a filter. Let your thoughts to freely flow.
5. Try a new recipe. It could be a Pinterest WIN.
6. Write a thank you letter to a friend.

7. Set the timer, close your eyes, and breathe deeply for five minutes.

8. Turn on your favorite playlist -- turn it all the way up and clean your house - it's a great stress reliever!

9. Sit outside and breathe fresh air.

10. Re-read something that has been especially encouraging to you.

11. Go to bed an hour early.

12. Say "Yes" to something you'd really like to do!

13. Watch the sunset. Watch the sunrise

14. Listen to soothing music while basking in a hot bubble bath with candles.

15. Give yourself permission to say "No" to something you really don't have time for or are not interested in.

16. Have a mom posse date. Just the moms. Vent. Chat. Share stories. Laugh. Connect.

17. Netflix and chill. With yourself.

18. Go to a park, get on the swing and be free.

19. Buy your favorite lotion and after your shower/bath -- slowly and I mean slower than normal -- apply it to your skin. Paying attention to every small stroke.

20. Get up fifteen minutes early so you can linger over a cup of coffee.

Chapter 5: Give it up for the F Bombs

F-Bomb #1: Feeling

Feelings have power. A feeling is much stronger than a thought.

Feelings aren't facts though. They are indicators of your very own personal reality. Material facts may be disputable, but how you feel about the fact is not. And that is important.

**Feelings are how you perceive life.
Perception informs you how to live said life.**

Only you can feel what you feel. Others can't tell you what to feel. Your feelings are yours and you can have them because they are your own perception.

When I get on the phone with clients and the first thing I ask is, *"How are you feeling?"*

And I remember one mom would always say, *"Sang, why do you always ask me that, I hate that question."*

Her resistance to uncovering her feelings were intriguing to me. Because women, are taught not to talk about our feelings. Haven't you heard the sayings

"Keep your feelings in check"
"Keep your feelings to yourself"
"Don't wear your heart on your sleeve"
"Don't be so sensitive"
"It doesn't matter how you feel; it is what it is"

My question to you is …
How do you want to feel?

Happy. Sad. Inspired. Secure. Alive. Turned On. Calm. Relaxed. Energized. Peaceful. Authentic. Balanced. Strong. Vibrant. Sexy. Valuable. Healthy. Bold. Fearless. Free. Vibrant. Creative. Clear. Alive. Accomplished. Invigorated. Relieved. Passionate. Radiant. Powerful. Purposeful. Beautiful. Grateful. Masterful. Joyful. Magical. Loved. Enthusiastic. Connected. Aligned. Lighter. Nourished. Excited. Serene. Appreciated. Affluent. Energetic. Blissful. Confident. Rested. Grounded. Safe. Sensual. Accepted. Validated. Worry-free.

Everything we do is driven by the desire to feel a certain way.

From what you buy, what you eat, what you wear, what you do, the music you listen to, your shoes, ---- all lead to a feeling.

And, sometimes the path we choose ... we are alone. Those you thought would be with you have gone a different way and things may not have gone how you envisioned them. And the journey can feel quite lonely, as if the world is going to crash all around you ... I invite you to stop, look around, take inventory of your accomplishments ... turn every negative feeling into a positive feeling ... turn on some music that fits your mood and allow your feelings to move through every inch of your being.

Give yourself permission to feel. Embrace the journey of emotions and, my hope, is that you walk away with a sense of fulfillment to continue to showcase your brilliance to the world just as you are and on the path that you have chosen.

F-Bomb #2: Forgive

On Forgiving Men

Man oh Man.

When I went through the *School of Womanly Arts*, my biggest forgiveness was around men. I did not realize how much of an impact all the men had on my life. There was so much pain. Lots of tears. Broken heart. Shattered dreams. Diminishing self-worth.

I had to learn to address what I never spoke about without judgement. I felt like damaged goods. I felt like no one would ever love me. I felt like I was not worthy. I felt like my legendary love was going to escape me.

In order for me to navigate through those feelings -- I had to forgive. My forgiveness came in the form of a letter to all the men who had ever *"damaged"* me. I turned every negative event into a positive outcome.

Thank you for not paying any child support all those years because you allowed me to survive, thrive, and show the kid's what loyalty, strength, and perseverance looks like.

Thank you for molesting me in the 5th grade; you showed me how to stand up for myself and educate my children about men like you.

Thank you for always cheating on me because of you I learned to love myself unconditionally.

Thank you for not loving me enough or when it was convenient; you taught me that I am a Queen and should never be treated less than.

Thank you for never telling me you are proud of me; you proved to me that I did not need outside validation to own my worth.

Thank you for being the 1st guy to break my heart; you showed me exactly how strong my heart could be.

Thank you for letting your father make sexual comments to me; you showed me that not all men are protectors and I am the one who teaches others how I deserve to be treated.

Thank you for raping me in college, lying to me about happened, and shaming me to everyone; you gave me a voice to help other women speak up.

Thank you for treating me like an outcast in high school because of you I learned that different is my normal.

Thank you *for showing me that my "daddy" issues are a strength and not a weakness.*

Thank you *for treating me like a sex object because you taught me to love my body, take care of my body, and honor my body.*

Thank you *for taking me to the movies every Sunday and holding me in your arms; you showed me what it felt like to be adored for who I was not for my body.*

Thank you *for saying those wonderful things to me in college; you gave the confidence and courage to be the woman I am today because of your kind heart and sexy voice that replays in my head when I need it most.*

Thank you *for NOT having sex with me when I was drunk; you showed me that there are men out there who are gentlemen with morals and values.*

Thank you *for loving me so hard that eventually my heart shattered into a million pieces when our worlds collapsed; you gave the courage to stand on my own, be who I am without apology, and realize deep down — I am worthy of love.*

Thank you! Thank you! Thank you! *For allowing me to unleash my inhibitions, truly love who I am inside and out, move past all the hindering thoughts that kept me up at night, giving myself permission to live my life the way I ultimately desire, — because you truly helped me become the woman I am today.*

On Forgiving Myself

Allow me to share a journal entry.

Here we are defying odds and doing the impossible yet. Something is off.

How did I get here? It's not a bad place. It's a place of stuckness. It's a place of avoidance. It's a place of transition. Maybe the question is not how I got here but now that I know I am here what is the next logical and life for filling step.

The transition is real.

For me, I'm stuck in being seen. How do I balance love and business? And what does that life look like? How do I keep my insecurities from creeping in and messing with my head? WTF is really happening. How do I know I keep expanding my explorations? How do I communicate better? How do I get what I ultimately desire and that is -- for my legendary love to be my husband?

Oh my mind flooded with so many damn thoughts and my emotions have me paralyzed right now. No action. No movement. No progress. Just stuck. WHY? What are these feelings? Let's see

Overwhelming. Sadness. Happiness. Confused. Love. Tired. Restless. Unloved. Nurturing. Lost. Angry. Scared. Nervous. Full of fear.

I think I should define those feelings individually to see what arises from within. Where do they even come from?

I've come too far to give up. I've worked all my life for happiness. I've busted my ass my entire life and I am not able to ask for what I want. What do I want? What do I desire? What would fulfill my world beyond my wildest dreams?

Anger.

I'm angry at myself for not being enough. I'm angry at myself for not having enough.
I'm angry at myself for not having financial security. I'm angry at myself
for not being smart with money.
I'm angry at myself for not showing up for me.
I'm angry at myself for not working hard enough. I'm angry at myself for not giving for not having a real foundation for my kids.
I'm angry at myself for not following my dreams early on.
I'm angry at myself for not committing to myself and Michael's and my dreams.
I'm angry at myself for not allowing to be loved.
I'm angry at myself for not knowing how to ask for what I want.
I'm angry at myself for not knowing for not being smarter than I am.
I'm angry at myself for being a hypocrite.
I'm angry at myself for not standing up for myself.
I'm angry at myself for not providing more for my kids.
I'm angry at myself that I cannot fucking be responsible adult.
I'm angry at myself for not making sure foundational pieces are always taken care of.
I'm angry at myself for not teaching my kids more.
I'm angry at myself for not having traditions as my kids got older.

I'm angry at myself for not being a better mother to them. I'm angry at myself for not being a better sister to my siblings. I'm angry at myself for not holding family as valuable as I did as a child.
I'm angry at myself for being a grown ass woman who is an enough.
I'm angry at myself for not having more than what I have now.
I'm angry at myself for giving too much. I'm angry at myself for saying silent.
I'm angry at myself for not being consistent.
I'm angry at myself for not being for not loving myself sooner.
I'm angry at myself for not saying what the fuck happiness is.
I'm so fucking angry at myself.
I'm angry at myself for not seeing this sooner.

Why was I so angry? What was going on? I needed to forgive myself to heal from those penetrating thoughts that were paralyzing me.

Self-forgiveness is the most phenomenal freedom and all love flows right there from the core of your own forgiveness. Forgiveness is our ultimate responsibility to others because when you forgive yourself everyone implicated in the painful situation is liberated in some way.

And you deserve to let go of your grudges against yourself because forgiveness allows you to cut the energetic hold that is preventing you from taking action. Be free from what is holding you back

You and I both know that we can sometimes be hard on ourselves.

And we often contribute in the bruises we receive from the outside world by punching ourselves with self-judgment. We chastise ourselves for putting ourselves in harm's way. I shouldn't have done that. I shouldn't have been there. I should've been smarter. I should've been stronger. I should've known better. I should've been less sensitive. I should've listened more.

What we project, we perceive, what we see and really determines what we see outside of our mind.

... and sometimes those should have been true. However, we must still forgive ourselves. I forgive myself for not being stronger I forgive myself for not knowing better I forgive myself for not being sensitive I forgive myself for not being smarter or stronger or wiser. I forgive myself for being there

All is forgiven.
When you're ready.

Power & Pleasure Playground

Say what you really feel. No filter.
Grab a journal, use your notes app on your phone and everyday - begin to write down everything you wanted to say but did not say and how you felt.

Examples would be:

I wish my kids would go to their room and leave me the hell alone. I feel trapped.

Gosh. I wish people would mind their own business and stay out of mine.

The people I work are the most judgmental bitches ever.

Use this tool to navigate through the feelings that come up for you and how you wish to handle it vs. how you actually handle it. At the end of the week, take a moment to reflect what happened and determine how you want to shift things that are more in your pleasure wheel.

The first two steps and forgiveness

Step one. Forgive yourself for not wanting to forgive.

> Anger feels so right. And being right can feel powerful. And in powering feels like it's the right thing. And it's OK. Because really who wants to forgive?

> So, we start there. I don't want to forgive him because ________. I forgive myself for not wanting to forgive.

Step two. Have a desire to forgive.

> That's it. You don't necessarily have to forgive you don't have to have a date when you're going to forgive just know that in your heart you want to forgive just wanting to forgive is the first step.

Write Yourself a Letter

> Dear Self,

> *Today I let myself off the hook. I look upon my life experience of the living I. I forgive myself for all my fearful thoughts and actions. I know that when I let go of my anger and self-sabotage and self-attack, I will recalibrate my loving presence from within. I forgive myself. I'm clearing space for loving guidance to be welcome in. Today, forgiveness is my primary function.*

> Love, Me

THE LIFE SECTION

Village: a self-contained community within a city or town
Posse: *a group of people who have a common characteristic or purpose.* ***Choose wisely.***

Chapter 6: Beware of the "Village"

This is the shortest chapter of the entire because it is cut and dry.

You know the cliché saying, "It takes a village ... blah blah blah" well I called BS on that "village" nonsense. In 2015 my son was making decisions there were against the rules of the house and I decided to ask another mom for some specific activities regarding my child. When I asked her about what happened and who all was involved -- her response was, *"I don't feel comfortable telling you because their parents will get mad."*

I promise you I was like a deer in headlights.

Like WHAT? YOU ARE JOKING RIGHT?
  she was dead serious

I had questioned this "village" business before and now my decision was firm. EFF THE SOCIETAL "VILLAGE"! I NEED A MOTHER FUCKIN' POSSE!

According to good ole Webster, the definition of a posse is, *"a body of men, typically armed, summoned by a sheriff to enforce the law."*

To me, the posse is a group people who have your back no matter what and will stand by you, whatever your decision you make.

"Look, here's the deal. I don't need y'all to approve my choices, alright? But I do ask you to respect them."
~Leigh Anne Touhy, The Blind Side

And so I made sure I had a Mom Posse which comprised of a group of moms that were ride or die type of moms -- they get you - you get them - they know how you parent - they respect that - they hold you down - they lift you up - they have your back - you can tell them anything -- free of judgement ... end of story.

Call them what you want. Inner Circle. Your Tribe. Mom Squad.

Whatever you do, create the support system that gives you pleasure (and an extra side of sanity).

Chapter 7: Feel Good About Your Money

DISCLAIMER

I am not an expert on money at all. I am only sharing how I have kept my money sanity as a Single Mother raising kids who were super active in competitive dance, baseball, football and so on. I became a master of moving my money in a way to work for me. And it became exhausting.

Here is the truth about this chapter, it is not going to solve all of your money issues. It would be wonderful, if upon reading this chapter, you went straight into ultimate financial security. Remember when I told you everyone's journey is different, well, our money stories are different too.

From what we were taught about money to how we teach our children about money. Society likes to keep Single Mothers in a constant state of money scarcity mode.

I remember being on welfare and receiving cash assistance, daycare assistance, rental assistance, and food stamps. And I could never figure out how I was ever going to get off of welfare. Because every time I had a job making minimum wage, I lost so much many benefits from the state that I was constantly struggling. It was a vicious cycle that I had to get out of somehow.

After working job after job after job, I had to get some financial education. And, unfortunately, my financial education came in the form of sexual harassment and a scam.

Some companies prey on Single Mothers so that they can give them this pipe dream about money, the "NOW MONEY NOW" facade and that everything is gonna be OK as long as they listen to what they say. They offer these band-aid solutions when it comes to money and finances and at the end of the program - you are worse off than you were before. And these companies REALLY piss me up because it's pathetic.

STAY AWAY FROM THEM.

Question everything. Never feel like you don't deserve to know what you want to know about money and if the vibes don't feel good. RUN.

And I get it. I have been that Single Mom. I was "sold" the hope dream of making $$$$ money in the next 30 days and it's going to keep getting better. Only to fall on my face one day 31, be super angry at myself and back on the struggle train.

It's hard not to want to make some quick money to get out of a money situation and those marketers do a REALLY good job of reeling you in. Sometimes those money situations are only $100 - but that $100 feels like $10,000 to make, ya know?

After coaching thousands of Single Mothers, here are the most popular money truths:

#MoneyTruth
Dick does not pay the bills.

I promise if you called the electric company to pay the light bill with some dick – it is not going to work. Now. If it does, call me so I can move where you are. Stay focused on your money goals. Get your money stuff together first, then worry about the men.

#MoneyTruth
Money survivor mentality mode is not sexy at all.

All throughout the kids' lives, they did not go without. They traveled with their competitive baseball, football, dance and whatever. I made a promise to give my kids a many experience as I could, but I tell you there were tons of times when I was barely scraping by.

#MoneyTruth
Money is my lover.

YES! I love money and money loves me. Money comes to me with grace and ease and in abundance. Become one with your money. Love your money as it comes in and love it as it goes out. There is more where that came from and you are more than worthy to receive it.

#MoneyTruth
Money doesn't buy happiness, it buys the
feeling of less stress.

It's not the feeling of happiness you are chasing when it
comes to having enough money, it's the feeling of not
being overwhelmed and stressed out and happiness
comes by default. I encourage you to get a jump start on
your financial education and DO NOT wait until you are in
a financial crisis. It is way more stressful then.

#MoneyTruth
Some months are easy and other
months are hard AF.

There is no harder truth than this and this is when the
power of your mind comes into play. Some months you
will hit every financial goal you set and other times, you
are tired, and you just wish money would fall into your
lap. It's human nature, it's normal.

#MoneyTruth
Single Mothers are not financially
ignorant. Society is.

We, women, are never been taught truly how to manage
our money in a smart way. We don't understand what it
means be smart. Road maps are kinda there, but do we
ever make it to the final destination? Typically, there are
no role models for us to mimic. And society has taught us
about money without actually teaching us about money.

Raise your hand if money is the #1 stressor in your life as a Single Mother.

Not making enough money.
Having more bills at the end of the month than money.

It's stressful.
It is not a lot of fun.
It does not feel good.
And being stressed about money is frustrating - at best and, often times, debilitating.

Not having enough money limits your choices, your freedom, and most importantly your peace of mind and quality-of-life.

Raise your hand if you just want to make it through ONE month with no money worries.

I encourage you to take baby steps. It's definitely a gradual process and money mindset training to get you on the path that feels good to you.

Then one day I came across ***Get Rich Lucky Bitch by Denise Duffield-Thomas*** and it changed my money mindset tremendously. One small step at a time.

Then I got my hands on ***I Will Teach You to be Rich by Ramit Sethi*** and things began to flow in a smooth money motion. I have the audio version too because the way he tells the story made the lessons more memorable for me.

My desire is for you to create the financial security that fits your family and feels good to you.

Explore your blocks and barriers around money on the power and pleasure playground. And remember ...

You CAN have financial freedom.
You DO NOT need a lot of money to get started.
Please don't wait until you are in a financial crisis to start.
And I'm rooting for you!

Power & Pleasure Playground

Where are you right now?
This is going to sound really stressful. But I promise you it works. I want you to get out every single bill that you owe, every credit card statement, medical bills, student loans, no matter what it is -- get it.

Then write down every single dollar amount that you owe and who you owe it to. Remember in Chapter 2 when I mentioned that when you need to accept exactly where you are and when you know where you are -- you are better equipped with the knowledge to make forward progress. This is part of the process.

Once you have that, acknowledge it and accept it. Then I want you to set that aside.

Write down your goals.
When you set goals, you're putting things on paper by focusing your attention to determine your choices that are shaping your outcomes. And attracting the opportunities to fill the gap. The clearer you are about what you want to achieve financially, the greater your chances are to achieve that. When you write down your goals, the more likely they are to happen than if they are just floating around in your head.

For some setting goals is a piece a cake. For others, it's pure heartburn. Remember in an earlier chapter when I said it's hard for women to ask for what they want or to write down? It's the same thing with money goals. We have it in our mind that we will never pay that off or have enough money for this or that. And if I had to guess, you're stuck.

That's usually because we're too worried about what everyone else wants, what everyone else needs, whether or not you're being selfish.

Decide exactly what you want. Then take action.

Create your own Money Mantra.

Single Mother Money Mantra
I love money and money loves me
Money comes to me infinitely and abundantly
I deserve financial freedom
I am confident in my ability to make money
I love money and appreciate the life it gives me
Money does not define my worth
Money comes to me easily and effortlessly
I am determined to get paid what I am worth
I am tenacious in earning the money I desire to live
my best life
The money that comes to me is a pleasure to handle.
I save some, I spend some
At this moment, enormous wealth and power are
available to me
I choose to feel worthy and deserving

Books I recommend focused on Money:
Get Rich Lucky Bitch - by Denise Duffield-Thomas
I Will Teach You to Be Rich - by: Ramit Sethi
Prince Charming Isn't Coming - by Barbara Stanny
You are a BADASS at MAKING MONEY - by Jen Sincero
Financial Recovery - by Karen McCall

This was the first book I picked up — ***Get Rich Lucky Bitch*** — and it changed my mindset with money, taught me about manifesting money and I read it every December after my birthday to get my money mind kick-started for the new year.

I highly recommend getting this book in audio format — ***I Will Teach You to be Rich by Ramit Sethi*** — his voice and the way he tells stories will not only make you laugh but you will remember what he says.

Talk about BUSINESS MONEY MINDSET — this is the book you want to get your hands on — Jen Sincero gives it to you raw and uncut —***You are a BADASS at MAKING MONEY*** — I listened to this book about 3 times last year and every time I learn something new. From here on out, I will be reading this one every year too.

I met Barbara Stanny when I was attending the School of Womanly Arts with Mama Gena in 2016 — and just hearing Barbara's financial story made me realize that I was very uneducated when it came to my finances. My parents were *"cash only"* type of people and were known for burying money in ammunition containers in the backyard.

I snatched every one of her books I could get my hands on:
> *Prince Charming Isn't Coming – How Women Get Smart About Money*
> *Sacred Success: A Course in Financial Miracles*
> *Secrets of Six-Figures Women: Surprising Strategies to UP your Earnings and Change Your Life*
> *Overcoming Underearning: A Simple Guide to a Richer Life*

Looking to repair your credit?

When I tell you this lady works wonders, it is an understatement. Contact Najah Walker at https://www.mycreditability.com/contact-us/

Schedule a free consultation with her and mention my name and this book to get a special rate. I promise you will not be disappointed. Also, remember when I said to write down all your debt -- bring that with you to the call as well as your money goals.

*"Sometimes I just want someone to hug me and say,
'I know it's hard. You're doing great. Here is some chocolate,
a blanket, and a million dollars.'"*

Chapter 8: Prescription for Daily Sanity

I've summed up parenting in three simple steps.

Step one. Provide your children with the tools and resources to make good choices to make good decisions.

Step two It's up to the children to use those tools and resources that you provided to them to make good choices and good decisions.

And number three. One day they will get it.

Because you say I always thought that my role as a parent was to prepare my children to be good citizens of society to make good choices to be resourceful and to be amazing adults. And not only did I want to be able to divide them with the tools and resources to do these things I wanted to make sure that I was not losing my damn mind every day.

When I became a single mom, I had no idea what the hell I was doing. All I knew is I wanted to provide a great life for my children and hopes that they would be amazing adults. I was all about teaching them responsibility. Accountability. And there were repercussions for their actions should they not handle their responsibility.

This chapter is one of my favorite chapters because I felt like I was killing it at this Single Motherhood thing with these time-saving, give me back my sanity hacks.

The Towels

Two kids. One boy. One girl. They both thought they needed to get a brand-new towel every single time they took a bath or a shower. Oh, hello millions of towels in the laundry. So, I started something one year before they started school. As we were shopping for school supplies and such -- we took a detour to the bath & linen section. And here is how the new towel process started.

Each child was going to pick out their set of towels. Two body towels. Two face towels. Two hand towels.
I empowered them to make a decision and allowed room for self-expression.

After they picked out their towels. I explained to them that from this day on, these were **their** towels. All the towels they thought we had ... were no more. They were responsible for washing their towels *(at this point, they have been doing their laundry since there were 10)*. They were responsible for keeping up with their own towels and every 6 months or so, they would get a new set of towels.

Whew. Talk about less laundry. Less water usage. More responsibility. More empowerment. My sanity and less to worry about. #SingleMomWin

The End of the Sock Monster

Anyone else have socks that disappear in the laundry and your kid goes flippin nuts because their favorite has been eaten by either the washing machine, the dryer, or they just stuffed it in their bed somewhere.

Enter the infamous safety pins.

I instructed the kids to grab the socks by their toes and safety pin them together and toss them in their laundry basket. Again. Teaching responsibility.

Because NOW. If their sock "disappeared" - it was not my fault as they were responsible for pinning them together. I relieved myself of something where I had no eyes ALL. THE. TIME. Cheers to another #SingleMomWin

The Kids Need Space Too

When the kids would come home from their dad's every other weekend. I would let them go to their rooms, unpack their clothes, put their stuff away and we would have dinner. I never asked questions. I never drilled them about anything. I let them come home and decompress from their time with their dad.

It was such a good way to give them space and allow them to breathe peacefully.

Highs and Lows

This is definitely something I wished I had kept up with as the kids got older and as we got busier. When the kids were little, we would have dinner together every Sunday or some week nights we would all be home to eat together. We would go around the table to discuss our *"highs"* and *"lows"* for the day.

Your *"high"* was something you wanted to highlight or brag about or something that made you happy or anything that just felt good.

And your *"low"* was something that wasn't so good for the day something that made you mad or made you sad or something it just didn't go the way you wanted to.

I created this space for the kids to express themselves without judgment and to share their day with me and vice versa.

The Code Word/Phrase

When my kids were little, I worked all the time. I had a full-time job, I had two part-time jobs and I volunteered over 40 hours a week. When you ask me how I got that done, I can't even tell you - but I did it.

And here is what happened. Because I worked all the time the kids would want my attention and I wouldn't be able to give it to them because I was working, or I would lose my shit by yelling at them to leave me alone. And my philosophy was I have to work to pay the bills - if I don't pay the bills - you don't get to do what you want - and if you don't get to do what you want then life sucks.

So, one day we had a family meeting and I sat the kids down and I said, *"Here's the deal. You guys are going to create a code word or phrase. You're going to use this word when you need to talk to me. You say the code word/phrase and I will stop whatever I'm doing and give you my undivided attention."*

My kids chose the code phrase: ***chicken and biscuits.***

Naturally the first few times they abused usage - as expected. But as time went on, they began to use the word for its intended use. I would stop that I was doing, look them in the eye and have a conversation with them.

What's so great about this code word/phrase is that as the children got older the code -- we transformed the usage into something different. What happens now is if the kids find themselves in a situation, a predicament or a place where they shouldn't be or where they're not comfortable -- they can call me up use that code word/ phrase and I would come pick them up no questions asked.

Why? Because they made a choice to use the code word/phrase as a safety tool.

There was only one time where the code word/phrase should have been used by my son, but it wasn't and that is a story for a different book.

The Trays

You know when the kids are in elementary school and they have planners or folders from the teachers. They want parents sign them every night and the kids get stickers or whatever. Well how many of you have forgotten to sign the paper or the kids forget to give you the planner?

Happens all too often. Am I right?

I created a tray system. There were two trays for each kid --
incoming and outgoing. They were responsible for putting
their folders into the incoming tray every night and I was
responsible for signing whatever and placing into the
respective outgoing tray. This way the next morning when
they were getting their stuff ready for school, all they had to
do was get their items out of the outgoing tray. They are
responsible. I am responsible.

Now. In the event that a child my son or daughter forgot to
put their folder into the tray. That is their problem. Not mine.
As you can imagine, that was a tough lesson for them to learn
because consequences are consequences.

YOYO Nights
Yo-Yo nights where deemed *"you're on your own."*

This meant that they were on their own to make whatever
dinner they wanted. I was not going anywhere, and they were
perfectly capable of making something for themselves. It
could have been a lunchable, a sandwich, a frozen pizza, or
whatever -- it did not matter. I deserved a day off from being
responsible for dinner.

To this day I practice a lot of discipline time management
and setting boundaries just to get my stuff done. Because --
just because they are older doesn't mean their responsibilities
change or my boundaries got looser. I still needed to make
money for the house, and they are still learning to be adults.

Now. What works for us right now, didn't work for us when
they were little. And what worked for us when they were
little, doesn't work for us now. As your kids get older,
whatever their age, you adapt to what's going on.

Stick to Your Word

The kids and I were in the car on a road trip either to Chicago or Texas - who knows - but we were going somewhere. And as we were driving down the highway the kids were throwing a ball back-and-forth in the backseat. I looked at the children in the mirror and said, *"If you throw that ball one more time, I'm going to roll down this window and throw it out."*

They thought I was kidding.

Because the next thing I know, there went the ball flying across the backseat. And I did the ultimate mom thing. I slung my right arm towards the back seat, left hand on the steering wheel, I snapped my fingers and said, *"Give me that damn ball right now."*

They gave me the ball.

And I rolled down the window and threw it out. Then I looked at them in the rearview mirror and, *"I said I told you not to throw the ball again. I meant what I said."*
The looks on their faces were like *"damn she was serious"* - and from that day on my kids knew that when I said something, I meant it and I followed through.

Let's talk about all the good things
And the bad things that may be
Let's talk about sex (come on)
~Salt-N-Pepa (Let's Talk About Sex Lyrics)

Chapter 9: Let's Talk About ALL. THE. SEX.

***WARNING:** This chapter contains very sexually explicit details and language.*

Reason #1 Why I talk about SEX

As a person who grew up in one of the strictest households that never talked about feelings, sex, or, for that matter, life -- I made a vow to open and honest with my kids with just about everything under the sun -- ESPECIALLY SEX. And if you ever ask them, they will tell you exactly that. I have not held back, and I tell them like it is. They ask. I tell

Also. I gave them a copy of this book before it went to publish, because I wanted them to know the stories, I am sharing about them. They approved. As a parent, I have always wanted to protect their privacy -- and I was super careful NOT to share any stories when they were younger until they were old enough to be approach.

I am not one to give out advice to parents because everyone's journey is different. Your path has been different than mine and we each have our own way of handling things and situation. Parent/Child conversations are no different. You do what you feel is best for your child -- because you know your child better than I do.

Reason #2 Why I talk about SEX

I never enjoyed sex for pleasure until I was in my 30's. I was sexually abused in the 5th grade and I was raped in college. I never told anyone about the 5th grade incident until my early 30's and, in college, I was blamed for being in the wrong place at the wrong time by the school administration.

My conversations about sex shifted as the kids got older. I wanted my kids (and still do) to make informed, pleasurable choices about sex, because sex is about pleasure. Enough of walking around telling kids that sex is only for procreation and only in the missionary position. If you're having sex, enjoy it. I just wish someone had told me sooner.

And probably the ONLY piece of advice you will ever hear me give is this ...

Have the Sex Conversations!!!

I tell everyone all the time, *"I was 18 when I first had sex. I had a baby at 19."* You figure that one out.

I highly encourage you to talk to your kids about sex. And if you don't want to -- I will. I feel it is so important to be open with them about a topic that seems so taboo. I remember, at the age of 21, I asked my mother what a blowjob was, and she told me to shut my mouth. Let's just say that I am still waiting on my mother to tell me. And yes, at 21, I did not know what a blow job was. HELLO! SHELTERED.

Here are REAL conversations I have had with my kids. They asked. I answered. Remember, you decide how you approach your parenting in whatever way feels good for you as a parent and it's OK to tell them you'll get back to them.

The shoestring

My son was about nine or 10 years old. And I noticed that the toilet paper and my lotion kept disappearing out of the bathroom. Now I know what you're thinking and it's true.

Yes. He was masturbating.

And I was the one to have the conversation with him. I sat him down and I told him that I was aware of what was happening with the lotion and the toilet paper and it was normal. I didn't want my son to think that him masturbating was a bad thing because it is normal.

I just needed to set some ground rules for the house. Because his sister was about six years old and she didn't know anything about anything. So, what I asked him to do to respect his privacy and to prevent anyone from barging into his room -- I gave him a shoestring. He was to put the shoestring on the outside of his bedroom doorknob and close the door and everyone in the house would know not to bother him.

It was a great way for him to have his space and her not to

barge in and ask questions I REALLY did not know how I was going to answer.

Son, it's called Blue Balls. Or so I have heard.

One day my son came walking out of his room doing a really painful looking crab walk. And when I asked him what was wrong, he said, *"Something is wrong with my balls.*

I may have giggled a bit. I replied, *"Have you been with your girlfriend and your dick is getting hard and then you're not ejaculating?"*

He said hesitantly, *"Yes."*

I giggled on the inside and I told him he needed to go masturbate or have sex to release what was in there and, from what I heard, it may or may not be a little painful when it comes out. And once you do that, you will feel better.

A few hours later. He returned no longer doing the crab walk and asked me, *"How did you know that's what needed to be done?"*

"Son, I just know what I know, that's all I can tell you."

Mom, what is anal sex?

I will never forget this day. My daughter was about 13 and we are walking into Olive Garden for dinner. And as the hostess was taking us to our seats and I'm walking behind the hostess -- my daughter is walking behind me and my daughter says, *"Mom what is anal sex?"* I thought the hostess was going to trip forward.

Now. Because I had prepared myself for these types of

questions -- just not at Olive Garden but because I had given my kids the space to ask questions - here we were. I went on to explain to my daughter how to have anal sex, what to do, what not to do, different ways to do it and I was perfectly OK with that.

I have received backlash from parents who found out I told my daughter how to have anal sex and I just laughed.

Because here's my philosophy. Because my own mother didn't talk about sex with me, I wanted to make sure I talked to my kids about whatever they asked. And in this case, I didn't want some man telling my daughter what she can do when he's probably never had anything in his own ass.

I believe the more my children are educated on whatever topic it is, the better equipped they are to make their own decisions on their own accord in their own way.

"Are you on your period or something?"

When my son was about nine, I was in the kitchen and I'm sure I was yelling or something because you know that's what moms do. And I remember him looking at me with a straight face and saying, *"Are you on your period or something?"*

I remember looked at him and told him to go downstairs and get the clothes out of the dryer and put them in the basket and take the clothes out of the washing machine and put them in the dryer and then bring them upstairs.

I needed some time to think. Because this is probably one of the first conversations I started having with my kids where I was really open about things.

When my son came back upstairs, I invited him to the kitchen table. On the table were Chips Ahoy Chocolate Chip cookies and some twizzlers -- the stringy kind. I asked him if he knew what a menstrual cycle was, and he said he kinda but wasn't really sure.

I began to explain to him what it was and how a woman's period worked. I used the twizzlers as the fallopian tubes and the chocolate chip cookies were the ovaries. I'm pretty sure I twisted the twizzlers into the shape of a uterus as well.

I'll never forget the look on his face. I'm not sure if it was because he was actually listening or that he would never look at Chips Ahoy cookies the same. Whatever it was, it's a moment he has never forgotten.

I asked him if he had any questions and he did ask what happens to the blood - did you just bleed all over yourself. And I laughed.

Because when he and his sister were littler, I would catch them in the bathroom going through my unused tampons pushing out the cotton and running around the house pretending they were whistles. And when I told him what they were actually used for -- he was disgusted.

Erectile Dysfunction *facepalm

Now you already know that this was not a normal topic of conversation. This was a topic that arose from watching TV. Because who openly talks about erectile dysfunction in their house?

When my daughter was about 10 years old, we were on our way to a dance competition one morning and we're sitting at the red light. And out of nowhere she asked, *"Mom, what is erectile dysfunction?"*

Now I want you to know that every time my kids asked me a question when they were younger I had to pause for a moment I had to take a moment to think about how old they were, what are they exposed to, what should I tell them, how do I explain it, and literally process the million thoughts going on in my head.

My response to her was, *"Let's go get this food and then I'll tell you when we're on our way to the dance competition."*

I told my daughter about erectile dysfunction but not after finding out what she knew, what she didn't know. Because to me the best way to determine how to explain something to a child was to find out what they knew? My philosophy has always been that if they are asking questions - they're asking because they are inquisitive - and, for me, it was about knowing what they knew too so I could either correct that knowledge add value to what they already knew.

Self-Pleasure

Now I told you the story about my son and his masturbation. Now I want to tell you about when I found out that my daughter was self-pleasuring herself. What I'd like to say is that she never asked me about it, so I didn't even know she was doing it.

You see, and I'm that *"cool mom"* that gets invited to the kids' circle conversations, dinner gatherings and such. I like to think because while they are kids -- I give a level of adult respect that they value and appreciate in a different way -- and I am not their mother. They also know I don't sugarcoat anything for them -- I tell them like it is, I called them out when they're talking dumb shit and I let them know how to best handle certain situations from a different perspective.

So, one day we were at an event and I was playing truth or truth with a group of choir high school students. Most parents probably would not approve but I don't really give a shit. The kids trusted me to be in our circle and I trusted them to hold the sacredness and integrity of the circle - after all, this was their game. One of the boys called on my daughter and he asked, *"Does your mom know you have a vibrator?"*

And she looked at him and said, *"Well she does now."*

The best part was that I wasn't angry about it. I was cool with it. Because, again, it's normal. Even though she and I had never talked about it she was comfortable enough with her own body for self-exploration to understand how her body functions and how her body works. I probably owe it to all the American Girl books I bought her when we would frequent Barnes and Noble.

And all I know, my daughter probably knows more about self-pleasuring, dildos and vibrators than I do.

This next story is a little different -- it's about me.

The Moment I Knew I Hated it When ...
… a guy would grab my hand and put it on his dick. I would repel. It felt dirty. Not once did I ever give in to that guiding deed, I would always maneuver my way out of it and touch his dick when I felt like it.

And I never know why until 2018.

I was driving one day, and it hit me like a ton of bricks. When I was in the fifth grade, I would go to a babysitter's house after school. And she had a son who was a lot older than me. Every time she would leave to go run errands or something, he would tell me to come into his room so he could "watch" me. When I was in his room we would sit on the couch and he would make me sit next to him. Then he would take my hand and put it on his dick and rub my hand up and down.

And that is why I was repulsed when I was being intimate with a guy and he would make this gesture.

I told my daughter the story not too long ago because I wanted her to know what I had been through and something had happened to me when I was a child had affected me into my adulthood and into my sex life.

I felt it was important to share this story with you as a woman who had a hard time navigating through her sex life. My hope is that this story gives you permission to, perhaps, reflect on something where you have built a wall.

Chapter 10: Create Your Ridiculously Ah-Mazing Life

And now it is over to you. I have shared with you the staple things that have been my philosophy on shattering the barriers of Single Motherhood. But like I said in the beginning, this is just one person's life, and one person's tips that worked and you may want something completely different.

I am always encouraging Single Mother to think for themselves and challenge the status quo. You're welcome to challenge or disagree with my way of living because we are not the same people. Dress how you desire. Define success how you see success. Stand by your beliefs. Continue to be strong because you are destined for greatness. I dare you to be different. I dare you to defy the odds. And I dare you to create a ridiculously amazing life that suits you. My hope is that you're inspired to be your own woman and claim your power as a Single Mother who means business.

I want you to direct your life, your destiny, and not allow the outside forces to control how you live your life.

As you may have gathered by now shattering the barriers of single motherhood is not necessarily easy. It's not about snapping your fingers and, in the morning, -- everything is fixed. It's much bigger than that and I hope much deeper. My desire is for every Single Mother to have a fulfilling and self-sufficient life, free of doubt, free of stress, free of debt, and as far from struggle as possible.

To have the confidence to change your life as you desire -- to dream a little bigger, to push the barriers a little more and obtain things society said you can't.

The overall theme of this book is you can do it by yourself – because you have been and now you have me to cheer you on. I don't want you to feel like being a Single Mother is a burden. As if there's no one around to help and nobody cares about what happens to you. I want you to feel like being a Single Mother is the best blessing and the best freedom you could ever have because you have the power to create that kind of life.

Please don't become complacent and waste opportunities for creating or even reinventing yourself as a Single Mother. Enjoy the power of self-definition and be free.

At the beginning of this book, I said I wanted you to live your ridiculously ah-mazing life. How you make that happen is not my business, as long as you know your value and hold yourself to your highest level of excellence. And as long as you keep feeding your desires of wanting more, being more, having more and shattering the status quo.

My hope is that my story as a Single Mother has helped show you that you CAN shatter the barriers a Single Motherhood how you see fit. Because at the end of the day, I didn't know exactly how I was going to make shit happen -- I just knew I wanted to be different and defy the societal standards.

Just look at some of the other Single Mothers who are living ridiculously ah-mazing lives. Sure, there are ton of people who had the means and resources to make their Single Motherhood journey smoother with support from their family and had all the perfect things along the way. But there are just as many Single Mothers who did not have any of that. Single Mothers who decided to be different and blaze their own trail of badassness.

If they can do it, if I can do it, so can you, but if you get caught up thinking they're too many obstacles in your way or it's too hard to be able to live the life you desire -- you have already defeated yourself.

Keep taking each obstacle one at a time. Because I can tell you from my own experience -- it's a difficult situation that you face that will define your character and who you are. The more challenges we face, the more capable we realize we are, and we begin to take every challenge head on knowing that you are destined to live the life you desire.

Like I said at the start. This book is not the complete answer to Single Motherhood. But I sure hope it has helped get started on the path to get everything that you desire and then some. I hope it's shown you that success often comes when a person prevails under the most intense situations. My goal in Single Motherhood has always been go against what society dictates I am.

My own desire to push the boundaries is where my strength and resilience has come from. It's a powerful reserve that I've put a ton of effort into to proving to myself that no matter what -- I can do whatever I want. And now I believe in myself more than ever. And that's what I want for you.

I don't want you to think that nothing bad is ever going to happen but that no matter what does happen -- you are going to be OK. Your resilience is evident.

I have no idea what your desires are, but I know you have them deep inside you. I want to hear them. I want to see you achieve them. I want to see what you're doing to move towards claiming those desires as yours and shattering the barriers of Single Motherhood as defined by you.

How does one bring closure to shattering the barriers of single motherhood?

The truth is -- we don't.

There is no "ending" to this book. That would seem like finality and the whole point is to get started on living your most ridiculously amazing life by shattering the barriers of

Single Motherhood on your own terms. Our lives as a single mother never ends. Even if you are whisked off your lover, a husband, or a guy who treats you fabulously. You will always have that inkling of single motherhood within you.

So, begin right now by asking yourself this simple question:

"Where will I be 12 months from today?"

Before you answer that question, remember that 12 months comes fast, and the following years will come just as fast. Soon, you will ask yourself, *"How come time just keeps passing me by?"* Please don't let that happen. Start small. One small thing can make a huge impact. JUST START!

It's time to start making your goals, your dreams, and your desires seriously. It's time to shatter the barriers -- go forth into the world -- and show them who you are.

It's **YOUR** time to shine.
It's **YOUR** time to **BE** everything you wanted.
It's **YOUR** time to **SHOW UP** for yourself.
It's **YOUR** time to step up to the plate of your **POWER** and create your **RIDICULOUSLY** amazing life.

Because … if you don't … **NO ONE ELSE WILL.**

THIS IS YOUR LIFE.

"The secret to change is to focus all of your energy, not on fighting the old, but on building the new."
~Socrates

Love Notes to My People

Thank you to my favorite son, **_Pretty Boy aka Isaiah_**, who made me a mother and kicked started this single motherhood journey. You have taken me on a roller coaster ride that, I have a feeling, is not over yet. Know that you can do and be whatever you want, and I am always here.

Thank you to my favorite daughter, **_Angel Cakes aka #TheDancer aka Angel_**, who has more confidence in her body than I have ever had in my entire life. You are one of the bravest women I know, and I am ecstatic to watch how the world receives you and your badassery.

Thank you to my favorite sister, **_Kimmy,_** who has shown me life lessons through her eyes. She is the mother who I always wanted to be, she is attentive, makes memories, laughs, and is truly the smartest sister on the planet.

Thank you to my favorite brother, **_Junior_**, who will always be my big brother. You've accepted me for my pitfalls and shortcomings and never gave up on me.

Thank you, **_Patouchka_** for the early morning calls, for wiping my tears over the phone, for being the person to rub my sunburnt booty in Miami - that is true friendship. I could not have completed this without your love and support.

Thank you, **_Katherine_** who is not only, one of the most gorgeous women I know but a woman who has reminded me of why I started this journey. I am forever grateful for meeting you because of my addiction to the Starbucks atmosphere.

Thank you, **Paula** for making my childhood dream come true in the world of pageantry. I would have never been a Queen without you. And for the parenting convos -- being a mom to a boy is hard AF.

Thank you, **Jennifer** for our mom dates, for showing me I can do life at my own pace and for reminding me that is it OK to want to shove your kid out of a moving car because you've just had it over your eyeballs.

Thank you, **Laurene** for the Spring Cleans, asking me the hard questions to expand and explore and for our perfect and divine timing. You're the epitome of sisterhood and I can't wait for you to be the one to marry me and my guy.

Thank you, **Regina aka Mama Gena, + Her School of Womanly Arts Posse** for creating an experience that fanned my buried desires that I knew were there -- just not exposed.

Thank you, **Sister Goddesses of Creation 2017**, for holding space, giving me space, listening to me, dancing with me and being the most divine sister circle, I have ever been a part of.

www.ingramcontent.com/pod-product-compliance
Lightning Source LLC
Chambersburg PA
CBHW050008040726
47599CB00014B/1280